CHICAGO BULLS

LUKE HANLON

Apex is distributed by North Star Editions:
sales@northstareditions.com | 888-417-0195

Produced for Apex by Red Line Editorial.

Photographs ©: Rick Scuteri/AP Images, cover, 1; Geoff Stellfox/Getty Images Sport/Getty Images, 4–5, 6–7; Bettman/Getty Images, 8–9, 12–13; Focus On Sport/Getty Images Sport/Getty Images, 10–11, 22–23, 24–25, 37, 38–39; Reed Saxon/AP Images, 14–15, 58–59; Jonathan Daniel/Getty Images Sport/Getty Images, 16–17, 28–29, 32–33, 42–43; Paul Natkin/Archive Photos/Getty Images, 18–19; George Gojkovich/Getty Images Sport/Getty Images, 20–21, Beth A. Keiser/AP Images, 27, 57; Jonathan Daniel/Allsport/Getty Images Sport/Getty Images, 30–31; Stacy Revere/Getty Images Sport/Getty Images, 34–35; Nathaniel S. Butler/NBAE/Getty Images/GDA/AP Images, 40–41; Jamie Sabau/Getty Images Sport/Getty Images, 44–45; Mike Ehrmann/Getty Images Sport/Getty Images, 47; Shutterstock Images, 48–49; Jeff Roberson/AP Images, 50–51; Matt Marton/AP Images, 52–53; Michael Reaves/Getty Images Sport/Getty Images, 54–55

Library of Congress Control Number: 2025939633

ISBN
979-8-89250-897-1 (hardcover)
979-8-89250-928-2 (paperback)
979-8-89824-004-2 (ebook pdf)
979-8-89250-959-6 (hosted ebook)

Printed in the United States of America
Mankato, MN
012026

NOTE TO PARENTS AND EDUCATORS

Apex books are designed to build literacy skills in striving readers. Exciting, high-interest content attracts and holds readers' attention. The text is carefully leveled to allow students to achieve success quickly.

TABLE OF CONTENTS

CHAPTER 1
SEE RED 4

CHAPTER 2
EARLY HISTORY 8

CHAPTER 3
LEGENDS 18

PLAYER SPOTLIGHT
MICHAEL JORDAN 26

CHAPTER 4
RECENT HISTORY 28

PLAYER SPOTLIGHT
SCOTTIE PIPPEN 36

CHAPTER 5
MODERN STARS 38

PLAYER SPOTLIGHT
DERRICK ROSE 46

CHAPTER 6
TEAM TRIVIA 48

TEAM RECORDS • 56
TIMELINE • 58
COMPREHENSION QUESTIONS • 60
GLOSSARY • 62
TO LEARN MORE • 63
ABOUT THE AUTHOR • 63
INDEX • 64

CHAPTER 1

SEE RED

Things looked bad for the Chicago Bulls. The Toronto Raptors led 110–106. Only six seconds remained in the game. Bulls point guard Lonzo Ball whipped a pass to Coby White. Then White quickly shot a three-pointer.

The Chicago Bulls faced the Toronto Raptors on February 28, 2025.

The Raptors fouled White as he shot. And the ball swished through the net. The Chicago crowd erupted. White buried a free throw. His four-point play tied the game.

In overtime, the Bulls took over. They won 125–115. It was a great day for Chicago Bulls fans.

RED CROWD

"See Red" became Chicago's team slogan in 2013. The Bulls wanted fans to wear red during home playoff games. That tradition continues today. Fans wear red shirts to games.

Coby White (0) celebrates after making his three-point shot.

CHAPTER 2

EARLY HISTORY

Chicago has a rich basketball history. From the 1920s to the 1960s, several professional teams played in the city. The Chicago Bulls were created in 1966. The team joined the National Basketball Association (NBA).

Guy Rodgers (5) goes up for a shot in a 1966 game against the Philadelphia 76ers.

In 1974, Bulls forward Bob Love scored his 10,000th point. He was also a great defender.

The Bulls made the playoffs in their first season. They were the first NBA team to do that. Chicago hired head coach Dick Motta in 1968. His teams always played tough defense. Motta led the Bulls to the conference finals in 1974. They made it back in 1975. But Chicago lost the series both years.

PRO OWNER

Dick Klein founded the Bulls. He had played pro basketball in Chicago in the 1940s. Klein was the first former pro player to become an NBA owner.

Michael Jordan reaches over a Cavaliers defender to make a shot in the 1989 playoffs.

Dick Motta left the team after the 1975–76 season. The Bulls struggled for years without him. But a new era was coming.

In 1984, Chicago chose Michael Jordan in the draft. He led the Bulls to the playoffs as a rookie. By 1989, Chicago was back in the conference finals.

THE SHOT

The Bulls played the Cleveland Cavaliers in the 1989 playoffs. In Game 5, Chicago trailed by one point with three seconds left. Michael Jordan hit a buzzer-beater. His shot won the series.

The Bulls fell to the Detroit Pistons in the 1989 conference finals. After that, Chicago hired a new head coach. The Bulls improved under Phil Jackson. But in 1990, Chicago lost to the Pistons in the conference finals again.

The tide turned in 1991. Chicago swept Detroit in the conference finals that year. Then the Bulls beat the Los Angeles Lakers to win their first NBA title.

Chicago players celebrate after winning the 1991 Finals.

Jackson kept the Bulls humming. The team returned to the Finals in 1992. Chicago beat the Portland Trail Blazers in six games. In 1993, the Bulls faced the Phoenix Suns in the Finals. Chicago won again. The Bulls became the first team to three-peat since 1966.

EARLY EXIT

Michael Jordan led the Bulls to three straight titles. Then he made a shocking announcement. After the 1992–93 season, he retired. Jordan played minor league baseball in 1994.

Chicago beat the Suns in six games to win the 1993 Finals.

CHAPTER 3

LEGENDS

Jerry Sloan grew up in Illinois. He joined the Bulls in their first season. Fans called him the "Original Bull." Sloan became known for playing great defense.

Jerry Sloan made the All-Star team twice in his career.

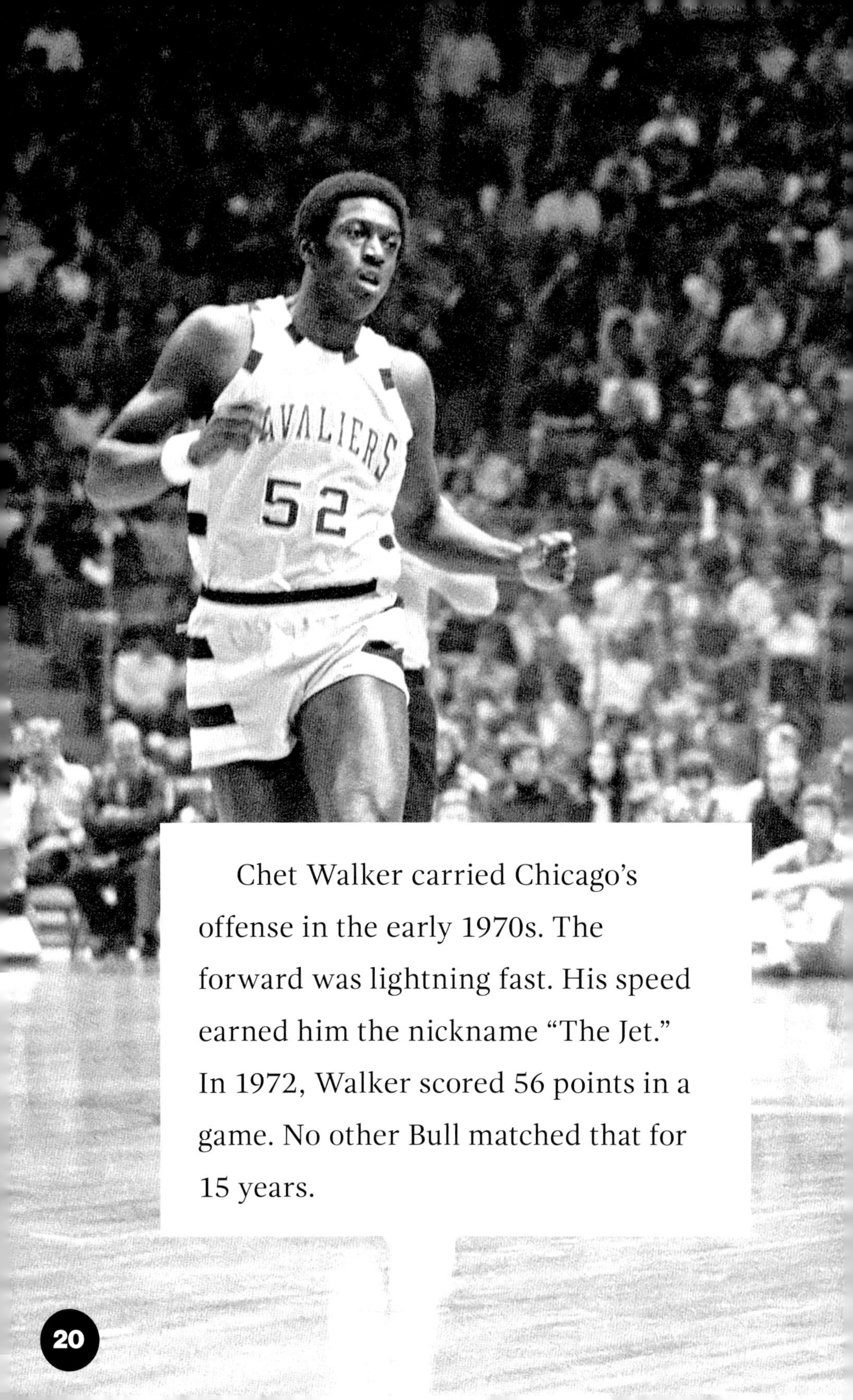

Chet Walker carried Chicago's offense in the early 1970s. The forward was lightning fast. His speed earned him the nickname "The Jet." In 1972, Walker scored 56 points in a game. No other Bull matched that for 15 years.

Chet Walker (25) averaged 20.6 points per game in his six seasons with the Bulls.

LOVE IN CHICAGO

The Bulls traded for Bob Love in 1968. He became one of the best players in team history. The six-foot-eight (203-cm) forward racked up points and rebounds.

Norm Van Lier was another key player for the 1970s Bulls. Fans loved him for his toughness. Van Lier spent seven seasons with Chicago. The guard made an All-Defensive team all seven seasons.

SCORING MACHINE

Defenses had a hard time stopping Artis Gilmore. The center racked up double-doubles. And he rarely missed shots. He led the NBA in field goal percentage twice with Chicago.

Norm Van Lier dribbles toward the basket in a 1975 game.

Horace Grant stopped opponents in the paint. He also grabbed many rebounds. The forward helped the Bulls win three titles in the 1990s.

Scottie Pippen was another key part of Chicago's championship teams. He could guard any player. And the forward racked up lots of steals.

CLOSER

John Paxson made several big shots in the 1991 Finals. He also drained a late three-pointer in Game 6 of the 1993 Finals. That shot lifted the Bulls to their third straight title.

Horace Grant averaged 8.6 rebounds per game in his seven seasons with Chicago.

PLAYER SPOTLIGHT

MICHAEL JORDAN

The Bulls had the third pick in the 1984 draft. They chose Michael Jordan. It proved to be the best decision in team history. Jordan's talent turned the Bulls into a major force.

Jordan could score from almost anywhere on the court. The guard won 10 scoring titles during his career. He also played fierce defense.

Jordan's skills helped him win five Most Valuable Player (MVP) Awards. And he always seemed to save his best for the playoffs. Many basketball fans consider him the greatest player in NBA history.

JORDAN EARNED FINALS MVP HONORS FOR ALL SIX OF CHICAGO'S TITLES.

BULLS
23

CHAPTER 4

RECENT HISTORY

Michael Jordan's retirement didn't last long. He returned to the NBA during the 1994–95 season. The next season, Jordan led Chicago to 72 wins. That was an NBA record. The Bulls won their fourth title in the 1996 Finals.

Jordan averaged 27.3 points per game during the 1996 Finals.

Center Luc Longley jumps for the ball during Game 6 of the 1997 Finals.

The wins kept coming. Chicago beat the Utah Jazz in the 1997 Finals. The next year, the teams met again in the Finals. And once again, the Bulls came out on top. They completed their second three-peat of the decade.

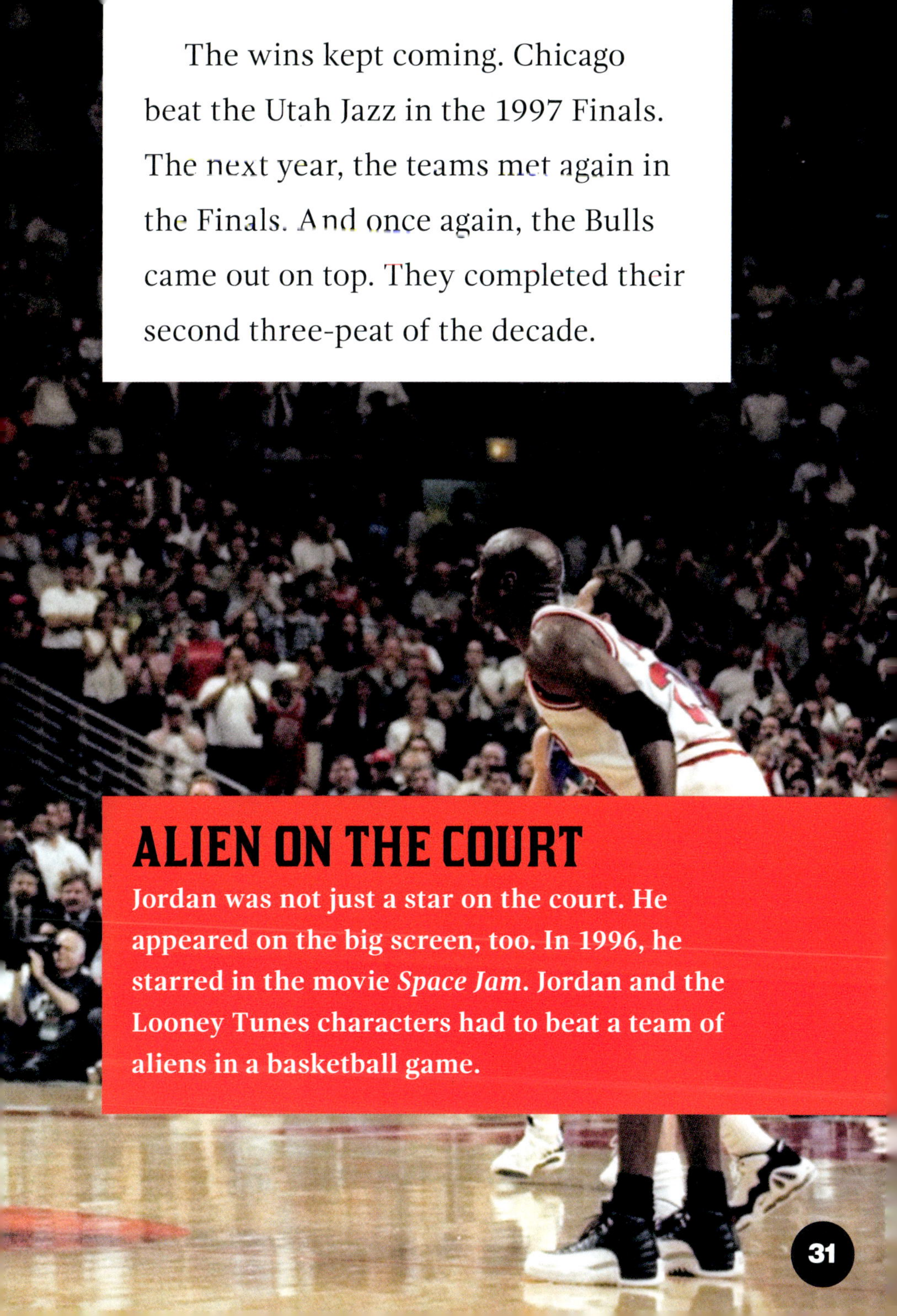

ALIEN ON THE COURT

Jordan was not just a star on the court. He appeared on the big screen, too. In 1996, he starred in the movie *Space Jam*. Jordan and the Looney Tunes characters had to beat a team of aliens in a basketball game.

Derrick Rose averaged 25 points per game in the 2010–11 season.

Coach Phil Jackson left the team after the 1998 Finals. The Bulls didn't return to the playoffs until 2005. Chicago drafted Derrick Rose in 2008. And in 2010, they hired Tom Thibodeau as head coach. He led Chicago for five seasons. The Bulls made the playoffs each time. But they never made it past the conference finals.

CRAZY SERIES

The Bulls faced the Boston Celtics in the first round of the 2009 playoffs. Four of the games went into overtime. The Bulls won Game 6 in triple overtime. But Boston won Game 7 to take the series.

Chicago went through a playoff drought in the late 2010s. Billy Donovan helped end it. The Bulls hired him as head coach in 2020. Donovan led Chicago to the playoffs in 2021–22. The Bulls lost in the first round. But fans hoped a return to glory wasn't far away.

Forward DeMar DeRozan scored a playoff career-high 41 points in a 2022 postseason game.

PLAYER SPOTLIGHT

SCOTTIE PIPPEN

Scottie Pippen played college basketball at a small school in Arkansas. The Bulls thought he was a strong prospect. He joined the team in 1987.

Pippen had long arms and quick feet. That combo made him a great defender. Pippen made his first All-Defensive team in 1990–91. He went on to make seven more with the Bulls.

SCOTTIE PIPPEN AVERAGED 17.7 POINTS PER GAME ACROSS HIS 12 SEASONS WITH THE BULLS.

Pippen did more than defend. He could score, too. Pippen helped the Bulls win six championships.

BULLS
33
BULLS

CHAPTER 5

MODERN STARS

Toni Kukoč came to Chicago in 1993. The forward was a strong shooter off the bench. He won the Sixth Man of the Year Award in 1995–96. That goes to the league's best bench player. Kukoč's scoring helped Chicago win three titles.

Toni Kukoč averaged 14.1 points per game during his seven seasons with Chicago.

Dennis Rodman (left) was known for his flashy style of play.

Dennis Rodman spent three years in Chicago. The Bulls won a championship each season. The forward led the league in rebounds all three years. And he played tough defense.

Michael Jordan played his final game with the Bulls in 1998. It was Game 6 of the Finals. Jordan hit the game-winning shot in the closing seconds. That basket sealed Chicago's sixth title.

Luol Deng (9) averaged 26.3 points and nine rebounds per game in the first round of the 2007 playoffs.

Derrick Rose arrived in Chicago for the 2008–09 season. He quickly became the team's go-to scorer. However, knee injuries limited his career in Chicago.

Luol Deng played a key role between 2004 and 2014. He thrived on both ends of the court. He could shut down opposing players. He also buried jump shots.

DEFENSIVE ANCHOR

Joakim Noah led Chicago's tough defense in the early 2010s. The center played with passion. He was named Defensive Player of the Year in 2013–14.

In 2011, the Bulls had the final pick in the first round of the draft. They took Jimmy Butler. They liked his defensive skills. But Butler turned into a great scorer. He made three All-Star Games with Chicago.

The Bulls traded Butler in 2017. They got Zach LaVine in the deal. LaVine threw down flashy dunks. He also buried many three-pointers.

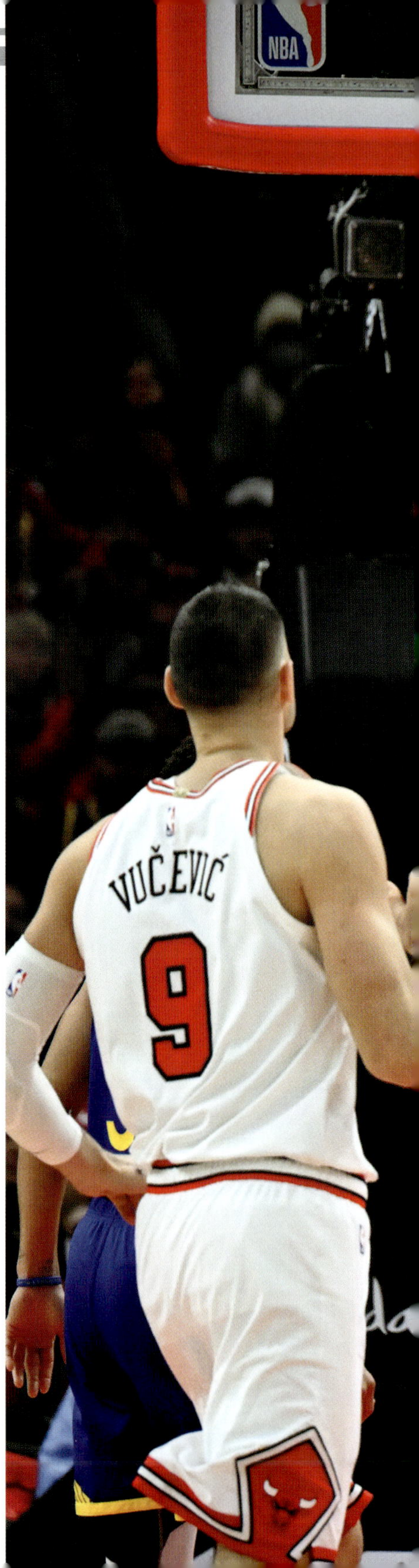

Zach LaVine dunks against the Warriors in a 2024 game.

NEW YEAR, SAME DEMAR

DeMar DeRozan hit a buzzer-beater on December 31, 2021. His shot gave the Bulls a win against the Indiana Pacers. DeRozan drained another buzzer-beater the next day. He rang in the new year with a 120–119 win over the Washington Wizards.

DERRICK ROSE

Derrick Rose grew up in Chicago. He entered the NBA Draft in 2008. The Bulls grabbed the hometown star with the top pick.

Rose took the NBA by storm. The point guard used his speed to blow by defenders. Rose won Rookie of the Year honors in 2008–09. Then he made his first All-Star team the next season.

Rose carried Chicago's offense in 2010–11. He won the MVP Award that season. At 22, he became the youngest MVP in NBA history.

DERRICK ROSE MADE THREE ALL-STAR TEAMS WITH CHICAGO.

BULLS
5

CHAPTER 6

TEAM TRIVIA

Owner Dick Klein came up with the team's name. Chicago had a huge meatpacking industry. The name "Bulls" was linked to that. Bulls are also strong and powerful. Klein wanted his team to be strong.

Chicago's meatpacking industry was based in Fulton Market. The area is still full of shops and businesses.

The Bulls were the first NBA team to use a mascot. Chicago introduced Benny the Bull in 1969. Benny still represents the team today. But his design has changed over time. Since 2004, Benny has worn a full Bulls uniform.

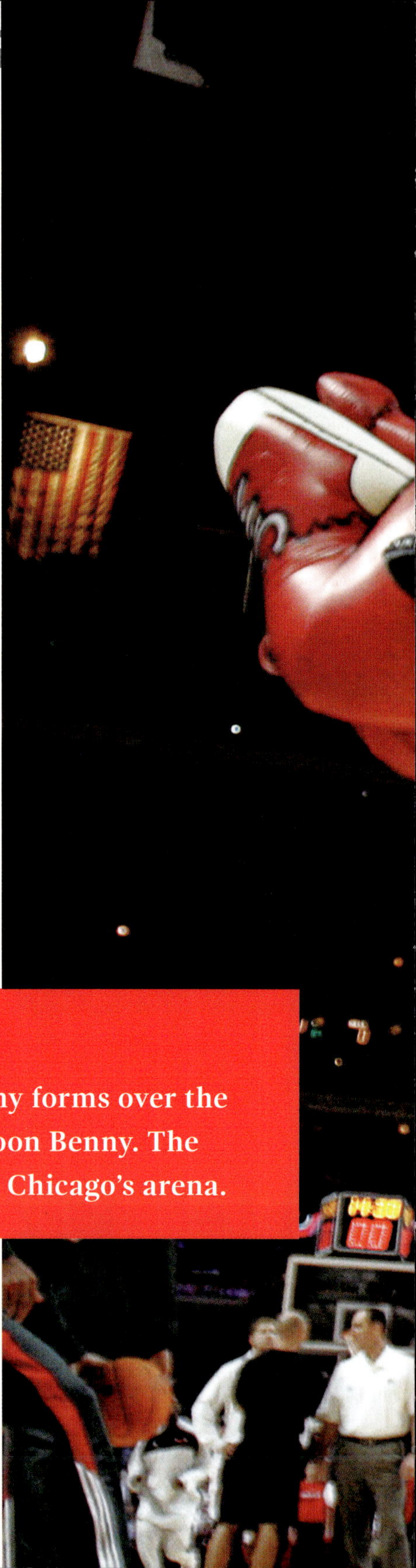

FLYING BENNY

Benny has appeared in many forms over the years. That included a balloon Benny. The balloon Benny flew around Chicago's arena.

A balloon Benny flies near opponents before a 2006 game.

Tommy Edwards called Bulls games for 25 seasons.

Tommy Edwards served as Chicago's announcer for decades. In 1984, he had an idea. He liked the rock song "Sirius." He wanted to play it while announcing the starting lineup. The Bulls started using the song that year. Chicago still plays "Sirius" before every home game.

RUNNING OF THE BULLS

The Bulls play intro videos at every home game. The videos excite the crowd. In many seasons, the videos include a group of bulls. The bulls run through the streets of Chicago.

The Bulls haven't changed their jerseys much over the years. In their first season, they wore white at home. On the road, they wore red. The Bulls still do that in most seasons. In 1995-96, Chicago added a black jersey.

GOING GREEN

In 2006, the Bulls wore green jerseys on St. Patrick's Day. Many people in Chicago are Irish American. They celebrate the holiday. The Bulls brought back the green jerseys for later St. Patrick's Day celebrations.

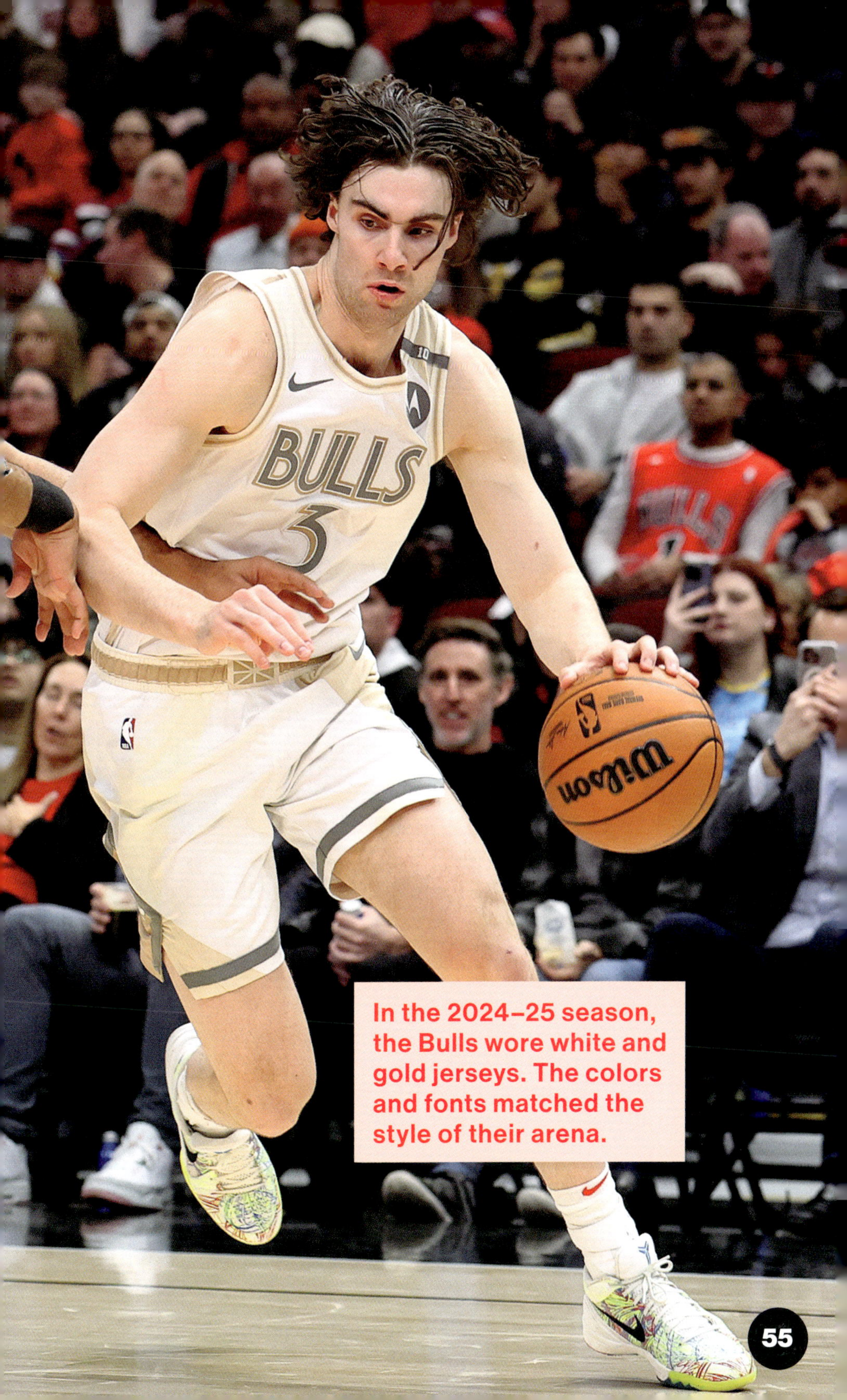

In the 2024–25 season, the Bulls wore white and gold jerseys. The colors and fonts matched the style of their arena.

TEAM RECORDS

All-Time Points: 29,277

Michael Jordan (1984–93, 1995–98)

All-Time Assists: 5,012

Michael Jordan (1984–93, 1995–98)

All-Time Rebounds: 5,836

Michael Jordan (1984–93, 1995–98)

All-Time Steals: 2,306

Michael Jordan (1984–93, 1995–98)

All-Time Blocks: 1,029

Artis Gilmore (1976–82, 1987)

All-Time Three-Pointers: 1,130

Zach LaVine (2017–25)

All-Time Triple-Doubles: 28

Michael Jordan (1984–93, 1995–98)

All-Time Coaching Wins: 545

Phil Jackson (1989–98)

NBA MVPs: 6

Michael Jordan (1987–88, 1990–91, 1991–92, 1995–96, 1997–98)

Derrick Rose (2010–11)

NBA Championships: 6

1990–91, 1991–92, 1992–93, 1995–96, 1996–97, 1997–98

All statistics are accurate through the 2024–25 season.

BULLS
23

TIMELINE

1966

In their first game, the Bulls beat the St. Louis Hawks 104–97.

1974

The Bulls make the conference finals for the first time.

1984

Chicago selects Michael Jordan with the third pick in the draft.

1991

The Bulls beat the Los Angeles Lakers in Game 5 of the Finals to win their first title.

1992

Chicago wins another title by beating the Portland Trail Blazers in the Finals.

1993

Chicago defeats the Phoenix Suns in the Finals to complete a three-peat.

1996

In his first full season after ending his retirement, Jordan leads the Bulls to 72 wins and their fourth title.

1997

The Bulls defeat the Utah Jazz to win their fifth title.

1998

In his final game with Chicago, Jordan hits a game-winning shot in Game 6 of the Finals to earn the Bulls their sixth title.

2011

At 22 years old, Derrick Rose becomes the youngest player in NBA history to win the MVP Award.

COMPREHENSION QUESTIONS

Write your answers on a separate piece of paper.

1. Write a paragraph that explains the main ideas of Chapter 4.
2. Who do you think is the greatest player in Bulls history? Why?
3. When did the Bulls win their first NBA title?

   A. 1974
   B. 1991
   C. 2011

4. When Michael Jordan retired after the 1992–93 season, how many full seasons did he miss before returning?

   A. three
   B. two
   C. one

5. What does **prospect** mean in this book?

Scottie Pippen played college basketball at a small school in Arkansas. The Bulls thought he was a strong ***prospect****. He joined the team in 1987.*

A. a player people expect to fail
B. a player people expect to do well
C. a player people do not get along with

6. What does **mascot** mean in this book?

The Bulls were the first NBA team to use a ***mascot****. Chicago introduced Benny the Bull in 1969. Benny still represents the team today.*

A. a symbol of a team
B. a championship
C. a draft pick

Answer key on page 64.

GLOSSARY

buzzer-beater
A shot made with no time left on the game clock.

conference
A group of teams that make up part of a sports league.

double-doubles
Games in which a player records 10 or more of two different stats.

draft
A system that lets teams select new players coming into the league.

drought
A long time without success.

overtime
An extra period that happens if two teams are tied at the end of the fourth quarter.

paint
The area between the basket and the free-throw line.

retired
Ended one's career.

rookie
An athlete in his or her first year as a professional player.

swept
Won all the games in a series.

three-peat
To win a championship three years in a row.

TO LEARN MORE

BOOKS

Hanlon, Luke. *Michael Jordan: Basketball Legend.* Press Box Books, 2024.

Streeter, Anthony. *NBA Finals All-Time Greats.* Press Box Books, 2025.

Tischler, Joe. *Chicago Bulls.* Creative Education, 2025.

ONLINE RESOURCES

Visit **www.apexeditions.com** to find links and resources related to this title.

ABOUT THE AUTHOR

Luke Hanlon is a sportswriter and editor based in Minneapolis. He's written dozens of nonfiction sports books for kids and spends a lot of his free time watching his favorite Minnesota sports teams.

INDEX

Ball, Lonzo, 4
Benny the Bull, 50
Boston Celtics, 33
Butler, Jimmy, 44

Cleveland Cavaliers, 13

Deng, Luol, 43
DeRozan, DeMar, 45
Detroit Pistons, 14
Donovan, Billy, 34

Edwards, Tommy, 53

Gilmore, Artis, 22
Grant, Horace, 24

Indiana Pacers, 45

Jackson, Phil, 14, 16, 33
Jordan, Michael, 13, 16, 26, 28, 31, 41

Klein, Dick, 11, 49
Kukoč, Toni, 38

LaVine, Zach, 44
Los Angeles Lakers, 14
Love, Bob, 21

Motta, Dick, 11, 13

Noah, Joakim, 43

Paxson, John, 24
Pippen, Scottie, 24, 36
Portland Trail Blazers, 16

Rodman, Dennis, 41
Rose, Derrick, 33, 43, 46

Sloan, Jerry, 18

Thibodeau, Tom, 33
Toronto Raptors, 4, 6

Utah Jazz, 31

Van Lier, Norm, 22

Walker, Chet, 20
Washington Wizards, 45
White, Coby, 4, 6

ANSWER KEY:

1. Answers will vary; 2. Answers will vary; 3. B; 4. C; 5. B; 6. A